1983

# MARCH LIGHT

# March Light

Ralph J. Mills Jr.

Sparrow Press
West Lafayette, Indiana

Grateful acknowledgement is made to the editors of the following publications in which most of these poems appear: *Another Chicago Magazine, Choice, Cottonwood Review, Dacotah Territory, Descant, The Madison Review, The Menomonie Review, The Minneapolis Poetry Journal, Mississippi Valley Review, The New Jersey Poetry Journal, New Letters, Poem, Spoon River Quarterly, Tar River Poetry, Telescope, Prairie Voices,* (Illinois Arts Council Foundation), *A Garland for Franklin Brainard,* (North Stone Press), *Richard Eberhart: A Celebration* (New England Review/Kenyon Hill Publications), and *Banyan Anthology II* (Banyan Press). My gratitude also to Michael Anania, David Ignatow, Stephen Berg, and Lucien Stryk for advice and encouragement.

Vagrom Chap Book Number 20
Copyright 1983 Ralph J. Mills Jr.
ISBN: 0-935552-15-4

SPARROW PRESS
West Lafayette, Indiana

# Table of Contents

## I

## II

*To Helen
with love—*

I

A stalled spring:
April is
done with
              and the trees
scarcely in
leaf
       their highest
branches whitened
by cold glossy
sunlight
              or shimmering
now
from a patchwork of
mist, drizzle
the small steady
falling—

              Struck panes
run with it, down
in rivulets:
              roof
tiles, this window
go dark
beneath
              as air stirs
the day's
grey scenery

TWO IN JUNE
—*for Michael Anania*

I
A dawn
wind keeps shaking
the maples
          sticks there
trying to
pry loose—

          And the leaves
let it go

               'Sibilations'
you might have
said: this whispered
breathing
          of day

II
Then the clouds'
splendor:
          large & puffed
bordered with
orange
          changelessly
changing
          luminous or dark

'Purpose'
          speaking only
for myself
          'to be
moving with purpose'

7/6

The sun's brassy
glare
        on metal & glass—
even concrete
                gives out a hard
white light
            though muted a little
by the wet air
            today
                so furred & heat-
burdened
            each step's in
slow motion—


            A life
narrowed down
            not to ritual but
some kind of round
                then broken
occasionally :
                say, by this morning glory
throat open & tilting
                up through
iron railings
            of a church fence—

Or driving north :
                masses of blue flowers
above a ditch
            purple bull-thistles, thick bunchy
weeds
        by the road's shoulder
wavering in the slightest wind
                    & past them
from a rise :
            fields in view, with their
green corn shine

A row of five
poplars
      bent as
one, crowns tilting
southeast
        Thin, supple
plunged in
sunlight
        to whom or
what should they be
bowing

       Only to storms
or hot summer
winds
      flinging them over
and back

        These trees I
hold to, don't lose
driving by—
        glimmer of
leaves
through the long
          cerulean
cloud-spotted
afternoon

BEECHES

This day, so hazy
and blinding
windless in July's wet heat—

Wasps, their long bronze bodies
hovering in sunlight
prowl the ivy
where it climbs a brickwork wall
and lie pulsing
on ledges

Coppery
or blackish purple
the rough leaves of beeches have swollen
to a cloud—
                    its indolent
shadow printing
the grass
leans gradually toward me

SUMMER NIGHTS

I

The afternoon greys a shade
each hour,
            lines of rain
edging north.

An air that's warm, burdened,
sleep heavy—
            small winds
push through the ash leaves,
the maples,
            a few already
rust brown in June.

            At the window
I wait for dark.

II

            Thirty years since
on summer nights at my grandparents'
with lamps off
for coolness,
            we ate or talked.
Aging elms
stirred overhead, scraping
the porch roof.

When the heat broke into
storms,
            trees keeled, rose again
like waves far at sea.

I stood looking
            and felt my arms
inside the branches
            sweeping down
and across
rain-drenched grass.

ON A WIND

I
A neighboring
bird cherry tree
lively
        with sparrows
almost reaches
this top floor
window

        Above the
grass
        a shadow-mime
at first light—
                leaves of
red maple
                playing
before a white-
washed wall

II
July days
spending again—
                the heat
builds slowly
                dampness
blurred to mist

Out walking
                I watch a
ribbed and
feathered
                longstemmed cirrus
it floats
past branches, leaf
thickets
                on a wind
urged eastward

III
A room, a small
cave
    the breeze enters—
shades flap
snapping at wire screens
and glass

      This chair
faces west
toward the dusk
        broken
flame-dyed
sky, greying roofs—

    below them
wild violets and white flowering
chickweed
      nod into
the hot dark

FRAGRANT FOREST
*(Variation on Max Ernst)*

The moon's iron ring
has caught
among stiff branches
bare of leaves

Here the gate of night
unlocks those
hidden glades
the pallid moon
can't touch

Water stirs, streams
wind beneath giant trunks
rivers are whispering
through buried roots
thick as lovers'
tangled thighs

Perfume of musk
of black loam
lifts in waves
toward the midnight sky
breath of a sleeper
haunting the forest
like a beast after prey

Somewhere above
stars could be hanging
jeweled eyes
but they're not to be seen
and the hand with its brush
has just stopped

              A baby
hawk/
          up
over the dirt track,
                  this old
bulldozed rail
bed,
        shrub, ditches of
stiff green reeds
                  & 'lilywort,
look' John said
                  his shoe
in the ooze—

              Feather &
tendon,
          wings stretched
in a glide/
              the Red
Cedar steady
              below
with its tufted
islands—

              Hand pointed to
round hills
nearby,
          leafless trees
black with rackety
crows—
                  but here's
where the scroll un-
rolls/
        words
out among birch &
white pine

SONG / FOR FRANKLIN BRAINARD

The respite of
thinned-out October sunlight—
clouds
        in middle distance
streaking and pebbling a sky
that's watery blue

Calm air
            dusted yellow
or gold
with flecks of red
                    where maples
surge into flame
        each lit
        on a short wick

What can be held to—
            grasses withering
            this dry fall
bent twigs   snapped
stalks underfoot

I kneel
        run a finger
the length of fine blades
summer has honed
                    and ease
over broken tips of
those dying
            here
fully in the moment
and sun

A night of wind gusting,
of rain whipped
until it pelts like ice.

In the morning haze
trees still quiver,
stripped down, skeletal
as their roots.

Underfoot, the leaves are
ground to powder
or bunched in a wet pulp.

Then a slow wedge of
sunlight, shadows
parading the grass.

Words lift on the clouds
of your breath: rich in
chill autumn, certain
and native of air.

YELLOW

I

Over against the dense green
leafage
of a locust tree
its yellow and blackspotted
scrolled pods
shaking
                    the grey tide of clouds
running high, heads
southeastward
                    broken now
and now again
by a bright spill of sunlight

II

Autumn:
the haze before dark,
air damp
as in August, still untouched
by cold—
                    but the trees
going brown, golden yellow or rust
erect above
their shadows, their first leaves
fallen to the grass

And the year drifts
—what
could hold it—
                    slips in the current
loose between fingers

this flow with
no moorings

III
A perfect half
of moon
when the sky clears

above roofs and the blue-
veined phosphorus
light of expressways

On my windowsill
one tiny
yellow flower
unexpectedly blooms from the
dark tangle
of an aging primrose

IN EARLY SEPTEMBER

I
Clouds like milkweed
tossed aloft
to the intense September blue.

This afternoon
I hear nothing but the locusts' buzz—
it rises and dies
through sun-flooded air
dazing me
toward sleep.

Now light wind loosens up
the maples,
a delicate ash too—
their restless leaf-fire
turns yellow to gold
and back.

II
After dark
the yard spreads
empty, dull
under the porch lamp,
the chairs taken in for fall.

A few branches of honeysuckle
thrash,
quarreling among themselves.

Unfamiliar faces enter my dream:
a voice advises
what must be abandoned in order
to live—

Nobody's there when I wake:
curtains unfurl,
rippling in darkness—

and outside: a moonless sky,
the wind shifted north,
its fine teeth
snapping off leaves.

A FALL SONG
—*for R.S.*

The cherry tree
crown's
        gone bare—

and sycamore
             maple
ash, then elm—

           with leaves
in places ankle deep
& stuck
        wet
to my shoe

        Soon, soon
a first snow
        ice-
luminous in the
thick half-light
        of afternoon
when the roads start to
close—

TWO POEMS

I
After chill fall
showers
      ivy climbing the
dulled rust
of old brick
      gleams
green as bottle glass—

And over chimneys, roof-
peaks
      huge blue &
sun-flushed
cumulus
      in procession
through a depth-
less clarity
      the air's own
while the wind
grips
      aimed along
a line from true north

II
Lights come on
in the trees—
    it's willow
    & the honey locust
yellow against
evening
   small fires
lit in this pocket
of dark
   I stare into

thinking how a leaf be-
tween leaves
    loosens
at the stem—
    in its veins &
    far off
the only message is
     snow

11/80

I
Not sudden dusk
                but a
late lingering sun
floods the ivy
                each leaf
face to the light

                its shadow
risen behind
   & painted black on the
pink brick
                the cloud-grey stone

II
No white clover
                little yar-
row or
        thistle's purple
left
in these empty lots
                nothing

        but a few
tasseled weeds & ghosts
of weeds
                spindly
bent twigs
                rooted under
& stubborn

III
           I stay out walking
while a hard wind
               crowds into
the elms—

           they buck &
    break up
in a rough surf of leaves
double-
toothed
        sawing the air

IV
Looking at old photo-
graphs today
         my face, yours
I almost didn't
know—

           The trees emptying
around me
        I stared through
clear to the bone

NIGHT SONG

I

Pale underleaves of
the white ash
ruffled by wind at dusk

A blackbird, cawing
flaps across the park

Far up
what light is left
greys, fades out
trailing a stripe or two
of purplish cloud
down the skyline

II

The moon a rind
stars gathered into wheels, rivers

or isolate atoms
flickering in the gulf

I rub the toothed edge
of a leaf
          and turning
wonder if I'm at an age when
I want to live
only in the past

Dry flakes of moonlight
sift
through the trees
                    unexpectedly
cold on my skin
as a first bite of November snow

ON A BIRTHDAY

Surfacing with the corner
ash tree
the sycamores, evergreens
into wet dawn light—

After three days
the wind has dropped,
a yellowed bone button of
December moon
hangs west, growing faint.

Rows of disheveled maples,
branches stiff with cold—
then near the park
                    weedstalks
motionless and brown
lifted
from snow patches
                    where sparrows
pigeons glide down
to scavenge
among wind-flattened grasses
and grey fingers of ice.

Forty-seven years—
a scattering of clouds high up
moves on
through an almost colorless
morning sky.

FOUR IN DECEMBER

I

December's fine-
grained
dry snow
pelts hard
across thick beds of
leaf and
withered grass

II

Red ash
          red
ash
beyond the window
polished limbs
quivering

III

Raggedy
sycamores too
in a
place I've walked
by
     some
still bearing
their rough furred
fruits
          with one un-
stripped maple
that rasps
chatters
to any wind

IV
Early light
          a sky
opening into rifts of
blue
          there
a thinned moon
tilts
pebble-white
in its diminishing
          and I
grow motionless
leaning out from my
shadow
on the sill

II

NO MOON

No moon
          not
one thin
rib of its hulk
left afloat—

          but there's a
black window
with stars
               an ash
tree shrugging off
air

     & somewhere the dead
in fading gowns
                    who
even now
               wait to be
dreamed of

14 JANUARY

From this window
the cold reaches of sky westward
swarm
with fierce roseate clouds

A year's wheel
has creaked round to beginnings
through rutted ice
                    uphill
into the wind's frigid maw

Smoke feathering above roofs
silver against
                    mauve
and delicate blue of the air
before dark

Recognizable in my dream
the January field
                    you crossed once
your black hobbled wing
traces of its shadow moving over snow

WINTERS

I

All night
I thought thousands of
cold, bleached moths—
unseeing, suicidal—
dove below the streetlamps.

I leaned over the window
ledge—
a narrow arm of snow
stretched there
and along each black branch.

Breaths rose
out of dead grass, the heaped drifts:
a cloud
hid my face
as if it were the moon's.

II

From a train
delayed among winter fields
in the Dakota night
my compartment window dropped
its rectangle of light
shadowless
on the flat snow.

I stared hard
at that unbroken whiteness—
far ahead
like a tethered animal
the engine was tugging and hissing steam
into the dark

AMHERST SONGS
—*for my sister, Anne Laurie*

I

High clouds are combed thin
over Amherst way
                    the sky's
wintery blue suffused with
sunlight
                    glazing ice on the Connecticut River
that snake-winds its valley
& shines


II

Down Main &
away from town
                    firs, thick-waisted maples
the air
greying around them
at day's close
                    Wind sways
                        only through
trees in front of
Miss Emily's homestead

Across the street
                    I pick up & pocket
this small cone
from a larch
                for luck

Near four,
stirred from a dream I can't keep
or reach back to,
I find an early February moon,
rags of smoke, chimney plumes
adrift on its face.

The lake stretches east,
a field of broken ice, slabbed and cobbled.
No clouds,
no shapes forming, altering
as in sleep,
only blueblack sky
and a nimbus of blurred silver.

At seventy, my mother says:
'How strange. Nothing changes inside—
you *feel* the same.'

I look down a thread of moonlit street
drawing its length under trees—

                    they're maples
whose dense tatter of brown leaves,
brittle, tinny,
grips winter long, beating out
sharp, infectious tunes
to the wind, the blown snow.

IN-BETWEEN

I

Almost evening—
the northern sky
            iron & violet
broken cloud off the plains
blown east
            wind
pitching the trees
                with now
& then again
                a quick grate of
                sleet—

II

At the shore-
line
        lake gulls scatter
        wide
& white as a
snow squall
                falling suddenly
above the grey-
green chop of waves
                they fish
a break-
water's tip

III

And

out of hard ground
    in-
between
            chips, splinters
of ice :
        pallid
blades & the frail
wavering strands—
                    these
                grasses standing—

BRIEF THAW

I
Winter grasses,
pale brown
and leveled under snow,
the black forks of
twigs prodding for air.

In today's sunlight
a brief thaw—
the sky arches,
flares wide, streaked
with cirrus.

II
Snow loosening
like shale
slips down the roof gables.

I'm drawn toward
the water pooled at curbs:
thin rivulets running off,
bits of ice
carried away—

Vein, bone, body
all afternoon in a light trance,
a haze,
moving to a high-pitched music,
the bell call
of seeping drains.

GONE

Rain sluices the choked gutters:
winter's trash
flaked with soot,
last month's snow spilling away.

Bare-limbed,
a maple leans its tough, spidery branches
into March wind.

Fifteen years gone
among roots and thawing grasses—
at the mirror this morning
I startled your face
staring into mine.

MARCH LIGHT

Into grey March light,
and air
barely stirring,
these skinny, twigged branches
of an ash
tug up
resolute, unbroken
by winter storms.

You look out at the shapeless
pillowing clouds,
a rainslick street below,
familiar
as this room where
you've turned around,
and again
round,
to arrive without ever leaving,
never to arrive.

But with dusk,
seeing grasses blacken
the years of wind have humbled,
you long
to wade among them,
plunging down suddenly,
wordlessly—
ankle, knee and elbow—

as into deep water
or beneath a covering wing.

Woken from a
doze
     to afternoon light
grainy as
sleet
     & thickening with day-
long rain:
        a smudge of ashes
thumbed across
street, trees,
        blank
wallfaces of city
brick & glass

     Yet
it's perfectly wind-
less:
     nothing stirs here
but water
     in which branches,
thin budding shoots
        stand &
are rinsed
     to a clear, tense
expectancy—

APRIL

I

A chill April;
Easter's moon swells its girth.
On a table, sleek ascending stems
of the lily
a friend has given—
                          two
have bloomed, furling back
wax-white petals
that curve perfectly:
                          a pair
of sculpted horns, the long
tapering necks,
throats funneling down
to shadow
out of which yellow pistils
lift in a spray—
                          motionless
as this room's unmoving air.

II

In yards, rain-
soaked hawthorn, chokecherry
press up green nubs,
the maples gleam almost
in secret, taut
branch ends reddening.

Now clouds pull open,
the wind is fanning slack willows—
still leafless
though touched by a green blur or mist.
I drive past, wishing them
already full—
                   wanting to stop,
walk in under a shower of branches
laden
and bowed to the grass.

SONG

Sunday
with the risen light climbing,
tracking veins of one leaf, another—
deep-lobed
silver maple, toothed elm,
tricorn of
English ivy laid along a stone ledge.

Far into the park
raw tongues of bird song
cheepcheeping, squalling
break from the trees.

What did
the leaves and grassblades sing,
blowing all night,
flooded by a white dazzle of moon
half silk, half shadow
that angled overhead?

For answer
a few clouds ride to the east,
strung out
above the lake's sunlit and
glassy water,
flickering
smoke blue
at the corner of my eye.

THREE PIECES

    I
A third day of
gales:
      the wind
hitting forty
or more
         bird cherry & maple
         nubs of plum
sprouting in April's
quick heat
         the dry air: dust-
laden, swimming with
grit
      clouds piled
southwest
         just before
a storm—

    II
The ground lies
         rain-damp
around walls—
         but though
there's no hare-
bell here
         blue-eyed grass
has sprung thick
         in a narrow
side garden
         mixing with
broken stone
brick
    in among or
under the bushes' wiry
coils
    & barbed twigs

III

Easter moon
        hung up
lustrous
        through the
undulant smoky cloud-
tides
        crossing its face

How 'sadly we
discover
        what we are—'


        Yet
these new leaves—
                silver & black
& of a
lunar cast—
                the air
                so much calmer now
testing them gently

THE RAIN GONE

Mist lifting
and the rain
gone—
        the sky's
diluted blue-grey
shedding its
last traces of cloud

Whatever the wind
tried
tail-lashing the grass
the trees
is finished for now—

        An elm limb
thick as a body
torn loose
lies in a scatter of
twigs and
small branches—

and I'm placid
adrift
at the end of a string
ear and eye
lost to the air

PORCH STEPS

I
This yard's one
plum tree
      flowers in red
the spear-
tipped leaves
         of deepest green—
or so they
seem in falling
dusk
     clarity of sky
a wood fence
dense warming air
          close around

II
Day
    drawn to
conclusion
       a little sun
burning an orange
fringe
     on the clouds
far up
     and soon
the stars flicker
in place, a moon's half-
lidded gaze
       drops
among branches of ash
their lean shadows
          woven crazily
over the ground

III
                    Standing
on porch steps
                    my feet
rise out of
shadow
            my own kind
of craziness
the moon can't see—

I'm thinking of Anderson
the balloonist
                    who spoke about
silence
in flight
            a dog's bark
slammed door
or wind
peeling off mountain rocks
                    climbed
to his ear—
                    He felt
nothing godlike
                    but suddenly
utterly small

IN MICHIGAN

I
Crows squabbling
through faint rain
         a mist
in the leaves—

         black-
backed shine of
wet asphalt
                  enters
the crowded trees

II
Roadside
by the woods' edge—

my daughter
finds there, in drab
twilight
         a glimmer
of bunchberry:
                  minute
white flowers clustered
         balancing on
long stems, tough
to break off

III
Clouds slip southeast
leave a paper-
thin shaving
                all of the
moon there is—

but still lustrous
silvery
            the lake too
which a quick wind
frets
        pressing tall
reeds in the water
to restless
                night-long talk

ALWAYS OPEN

Overheated, damp,
tonight's wind roots at ivy
spilling from its pot
on the sill.

Half in a drowse,
I watch the vines dancing,
listen to leaves
rattle, halt—then
shake again,
as if to tear loose and scatter
through my room,
the walls dim, uncertain.

Outside, the streetlamp's drifting
among blown maples—
I brood
on their patched quilt of shadows,

remembering someone who insisted
the dead you love come back
in sleep,
telling me a dream twice:
how with her mother and father
she laughed, joined a holiday throng,
and woke happy,
assured of peace—

The door, I think she said,
is always open. If you
go to meet them, let them through.

## FOR JAMES WRIGHT FROM A DREAM, 1978

I

'How do you know it's right?'
you ask, sitting
heavy-shouldered, while I
praise one of your poems
in a dream.

            I'm sure
and say so. We
talk on over coffee
of how the moon
rising
leaves a track to shimmer
along the Loire—
you trill the *r* like music—
its long finger of light
reaching beneath
the arch of each stone bridge.

We speak too
about your beloved Max Jacob,
who saw the Lord in visions on his wall.
Strangely, you tell
of reading him at the Chicago Public Library:
'They had two volumes,
in French—'

            Then my dream,
spun out, dissolves . . .

II
I think of you
at nightfall
gazing into currents of New York traffic—

But it's the Loire, or the black Ohio
where our bones go, and only a single
blue or white wing
lifts aloft
to sail into the trees, banked wildflowers,
and tall grass burning green
across the iron water
ruined lives lie down in and sleep.

FOR LORINE NIEDECKER
IN HEAVEN

*Lorine, Lorine*
*the catch is*
*in—*
        fish scales
crystal en-
crusted among the
wet grasses

House roof's
new-shingled
now, the walls
done all in
white—
        Nothing for
you but to
drift the river:
'a silent boat'
in this hollow of
green, leaf-shady
& still

But see, a visitor,
the sun has
come, dropping through
birches & firs—
                its light
spreads a band
on your hair,
                Lorine
the catch is in

GLIMPSED

Glimpsed from the window
before sleep—
                down
along rainwet
pavement
                where loose blowing maples
ash and a hickory
bow
toward their shadows'
black mesh
                as if inconsolably
grieved
                then pull back
trying
to lift free

—the small cube of light
in which I stand
                hanging still
                in the wind
above a frenzy of leaves

RETURNS

Days of fog
at the lake's edge—
                smoky white
in clouds blown down
over houses
                tatters
snagged in the leafing
elms
        & the sun
a colorless disk
that tries to burn through

Crabapple tree & cherry
have blossomed
                then shed
in a blizzard of petals
        the recalcitrant
ailanthus
                presses tight
                ruddy spikes
from each branch—

              Year after
year seeing them
slowly
go green
              above a backyard
brick wall
where sparrows gather to
chatter
              in a dream of
stems reaching
of lengthening grass
                            that always
returns   like gulls up-
river & back
to shore
              or light on my sill
after rain passes

*March Light* has been printed from Centaur type
on Ticonderoga paper during the spring of 1983.
Designed & printed by Michael Tarachow at
Pentagram for Sparrow Press in an edition of 500.